The Rocky Road to Civil Rights in the United States

An Annotated Timeline
by
Catherine McGrew Jaime

Books by Catherine Jaime

York Proceeded on (Historical Fiction)
Leonardo the Florentine (Historical Fiction)
Failure in Philadelphia? (Historical Fiction)
Sharing Shakespeare with Students
Organized Ramblings

Brought to you by:

Creative Learning Connection
8006 Old Madison Pike, Ste 11-A
Madison, AL 35758

www.CreativeLearningConnection.com

Preface

Much has happened in the history of our country as the races have struggled through how to relate to each other. Some of it has been good – much of it has been very sad. I have not attempted to chronicle everything along the road to equity between the races – but to try to hit the high and low points along that path.

As I conducted this study, several different categories of events seemed to jump out at me: "Society," "Government," "Military," and "Sports." These categories are by no means exhaustive, or exclusive. I arranged the various events in one or more of these categories in an attempt to more clearly show what happened.

I apologize in advance for any critical omissions that may have inadvertently occurred as I put together this little booklet.

I also apologize for my use of "whites" and "blacks" to distinguish between the two major races involved in that struggle, if that offends any of my readers. It is not meant to be offensive.

May we learn from the mistakes of the past – and try not to repeat them in the future.

"I have learned that success is to be measured not so much by the position that one has reached in life as by the obstacles which he has overcome while trying to succeed."

Booker T. Washington

	Happenings in Society	Government Responses	Related Military
1441	Portugal begins the European-African slave trade.		
1562	England enters the slave trade.		
1619	First slaves arrive in Virginia colony.		
1641		Massachusetts is the first colony to legalize slavery.	
1668		Virginia denies equal rights to freed blacks.	
1680		*Act for Preventing Negro Insurrections* is passed in Virginia. Blacks are prohibited from carrying any type of "weapons."	

	Happenings in Society	Government Responses	Related Military
1688	Quakers and Mennonites protest slavery in Pennsylvania.		
1706	Cotton Mather preaches in Massachusetts that slavery is "ordained by God."		
1721		South Carolina limits voting rights to white men.	
1739	Slaves in South Carolina rise up in the *Stono Rebellion* – sixty whites and blacks are dead before it is stopped.		

	Happenings in Society	Government Responses	Related Military
1775	Benjamin Franklin helps form the Pennsylvania Society for the Abolition of Slavery.		George Washington does not initially want to allow blacks to serve in the American military as they fight for independence from Great Britain.

Benjamin Franklin

Thomas Jefferson

"All men are created equal…"
The Declaration of Independence

	Society	Government Responses	Related Military
1776		U.S. declares independence from England. Against Thomas Jefferson's will, slavery is not mentioned.	
1777		Vermont outlaws slavery within the colony.	
1783		Blacks are permitted to vote in Massachusetts.	Revolutionary War ends. 10,000 blacks have served in the military.
1784	Quakers forbid member of their churches from owning slaves.		

	Happenings in Society	Government Responses
1787		The Northwest Ordinance outlaws slavery in the newly acquired Northwest Territory.
1789		U.S. constitution ratified – slaves are counted as "3/5's of a person" for taxes, etc...
1793	Eli Whitney invents the cotton gin – making slaves even more critical to Southern plantations.	Fugitive Slave Law passes – aiding runaway slaves is now illegal.
1799		New York passes an "Act for the Gradual Abolition of Slavery." All female slave children born after July 4, 1799 are to receive their freedom as they reach their 25th birthday, and males on their 28th birthday.
1808	Importation of slaves into U.S. is banned by Congress. (1/4 million will still be imported in next forty years).	

Slave Market

	Happenings in Society	Government Responses	Related Military
1815	Underground Railroad starts.		Black soldiers fight valiantly at the Battle of New Orleans.
1816	Colonization (in Africa) is tried as an attempt to solve the "Black Problem." The idea of sending black people "back to Africa" never really catches on.		
1820		The Missouri Compromise brings Maine into the Union as a free state, Missouri as a slave state, and bans slavery in the Louisiana Territory.	
1827	First "black" newspaper published in the U.S.		

	Happenings in Society
1828	When her master refuses to free her according to the New York law, Sojourner Truth runs away. After gaining her own freedom, she sues to retrieve her own son, who has been illegally been sold to a man in Alabama. She becomes the first black woman to sue a white man and win.
1831	William Lloyd Garrison, an escaped slave, begins his newspaper, *The Liberator*. He calls for the abolition of slavery.
	Nat Turner leads slave rebellion in Virginia.
1832	Garrison founds the *New England Anti-Slavery Society*.

William Lloyd Garrison

	Happenings in Society	Government Responses
1838	Frederick Douglass escapes from slavery – he will become well known as an abolitionist speaker.	
1839	The ship, *Amistad,* lands in the U.S. (instead of Africa) with fifty slaves who have taken over the ship. After a lengthy court drama, the Supreme Court grants the captives their freedom, and they return to Africa.	
1842		The U.S. Supreme Court rules in *Prigg v. Pennsylvania* that states cannot hinder masters from coming after their escaped slaves.
1843	After escaping from slavery, Sojourner Truth speaks out often in the North against the oppression of blacks and of women. Her audiences are primarily white.	

	Happenings in Society	Government Responses
1847		Dred Scot sues for his freedom, after being taken by his master into a "free state."
1848	The Free-Soil Party is formed, opposing the expansion of slavery.	

 *Dred Scott*

	Happenings in Society
1852	*Uncle Tom's Cabin* is published. It causes an uproar in the south.

Harriet Tubman   *John Brown*

	Happenings in Society	Government Responses
1857	On one of Harriet Tubman's nineteen trips as an Underground Railroad conductor, she frees her own parents.	Supreme Court decision: *Dred Scot v. Sanford*. Slaves can be taken into free states by their masters, since they are "only property."
1859	John Brown and other radicals raid arsenal at Harpers Ferry, VA, hoping to obtain arms for a slavery uprising.	

"Whenever I hear anyone arguing for slavery, I feel a strong impulse to see it tried on him personally."
Abraham Lincoln

	Society	**Govt. Responses**	**Related Military**	**Sport Events**
1860	Five northern states allow blacks to vote in the presidential election. Abraham Lincoln, who has expressed anti-slavery sentiments, wins the election.			A black baseball team, the Brooklyn Excelsiors, tour part of the U.S.
1861 - 1865	Civil War in the United States 179,000 blacks have enlisted by the end of the war.			
1865	13th Amendment of the U.S. Constitution outlaws slavery.			
	"Black Codes" created in the southern states, to control ex-slaves – everything from their hours of labor to property rights.			

"Negroes must make annual contracts for their labor in writing; if they should run away from their tasks, they forfeit their wages for the year…"
Example of a "Black Code" in Mississippi

	Happenings in Society	Government Responses
1865 cont.	Massachusetts guarantees blacks the right to vote.	
	KKK (Ku Klux Klan) formed originally in Tennessee by Nathan Bedford Forrest. It spreads across the South quickly.	

Nathan Bedford Forrest

President Andrew Johnson

THE FREEDMEN'S BUREAU.—Drawn by A. R. Waud.—[See Page 61.]

Freedman's Bureau

	Happenings in Society	**Government Responses**
1866		Freedman's Bureau formed to assist freed slaves. The First Civil Rights Act passed in spite of President Andrew Johnson's veto – grants citizenship to blacks, and ends post-Civil War "Black Codes."

	Government Responses	Sport Events
1867	Three Reconstruction Acts pass over President Johnson's vetoes.	
1868	The 14th Amendment gives equal protection under the law to black Americans.	Baseball's amateur organization, The National Association of Baseball Players, votes to exclude any clubs with black players.

	Happenings in Society	Government Responses
1869	Forrest is unhappy with the increasingly violent ways of the KKK, and begins to disband it.	
1870	The first Jim Crow Law passes in Tennessee, mandating segregation on trains.	
		15th Amendment gives black men the right to vote.
1871	The KKK disbands completely.	
1872		Freedmen's Bureau abolished.
1873		Supreme Court rules that 14th Amendment grants blacks "due process" under national laws, but not state laws.
1875		The Civil Rights Act of 1875 grants equal rights in jury duty and public accommodations to blacks.

West Point Military Academy

	Happenings in Society	Government Responses	Related Military
1877	First black student graduates from West Point.		
	Reconstruction ends in the south, when President Rutherford B. Hayes removes federal troops from the southern states.		

President Rutherford B. Hayes

Booker T. Washington

	Happenings in Society
1881	School for blacks started in Tuskegee, Alabama by Booker T. Washington. His goal is to educate black students particularly in skills and trades. Washington regularly speaks about blacks living harmoniously with whites.

"There are two ways of exerting one's strength: one is pushing down, the other is pulling up."
Booker T. Washington

George Washington Carver

	Happenings in Society	**Government Responses**
1882	George Washington Carver becomes head of the Agricultural Department at the school in Tuskegee.	The U.S. bans immigration from China for the next ten years.
1883		Supreme Court invalidates the Civil Rights Act of 1875, as unconstitutional in its limits on individuals.

	Government Responses	Sport Events
1884		First black major league baseball player – Moses Walker.
1885		First black professional baseball team formed – The Cuban Giants.
1888		White baseball players begin refusing to play ball with black players, causing the league to stop signing contracts with blacks.
1890	Mississippi disenfranchises black men from voting rights with outlandish voting tests.	

Moses Walker

	Happenings in Society	Government Responses
1892	Lynchings of blacks in the south reach almost epidemic proportions.	
1895	In an important speech in Atlanta, Booker T. Washington encourages blacks to work their way up from their post-slavery position.	
1896		Supreme Court decision: *Plessy v. Ferguson* – allows "separate but equal" facilities.
1898		Louisiana limits voting rights to men whose grandfathers were eligible to vote by January 1, 1867 ("the grandfather clause").
1901	Booker T. Washington dines at the White House with President Theodore Roosevelt, outraging many.	

	Happenings in Society	Government Responses
1909	NAACP (National Association for the Advancement of Colored People) is formed, after work by W.E.B. DuBois and other influential blacks. (DuBois was the first black to receive a doctorate from Harvard, in 1895.)	Jim Crow laws: Example: Separate parks in Georgia; 10 P.M. Curfew in Mobile for blacks.
1911	The National Urban League is founded.	

W.E.B. DuBois

	Happenings in Society	Government Responses	Military
1914 - 1918	KKK reactivated in 1915.	Supreme Court decision in 1915: "grandfather clauses" unconstitutional. Jim Crow laws begin breaking down.	U.S. is involved in World War I. Blacks are allowed to be officers, but not encouraged. More than 370,000 blacks serve in the military during the war.
1919	Red Summer: Race riots occur across America.		

	Government Responses	Sport Events
1920	19th Amendment – Women given the right to vote.	First black baseball league formed, the Negro National League.
1923		"The Renaissance," first black professional basketball team forms.

	Happenings in Society	Government Responses
1924		American Indians granted citizenship /right to vote
1925	KKK marches on Washington.	
	The Brotherhood of Sleeping Car Porters, the first black union, is formed.	

"Fight or Be Slaves."

Motto of the members of
The Brotherhood of Sleeping Car Porters in 1925

	Society	Government Responses
1931	In Scottsboro, Alabama, nine black men are falsely accused of raping two white women. The "Scottsboro boys" will suffer much on the way to proving their innocence, nineteen years later.	
1933		NAACP uses court system to start bringing about civil right changes.

	Sport Events
1936	Jesse Owens, black American athlete, wins four gold medals at the German hosted Olympics, shocking and angering Adolph Hitler, one of the chief racists of all time.
1937	Negro American (Baseball) League forms.

Jesse Owens

	Government Responses	Military
1941 – 1945	Supreme Court decision: railroad facilities may be separate, as long as they're equal.	U.S. involved in World War II. The Tuskegee Airmen, the first black military airmen, perform extremely well throughout the war, taking over 400 enemy planes, and not losing even one of their own.
1946	Booker T. Washington is honored on a U.S. coin – first black to be so honored.	

Booker T. Washington Memorial Half Dollar

Jackie Robinson

	Society	**Government Responses**	**Sport Events**
1947	Eight blacks and eight whites travel on a bus across the south to test the new Supreme Court ban on segregated bus travel. They are met with violent resistance.	President Truman addresses the NAACP (first president to do so).	Jackie Robinson, signs with the Brooklyn Dodgers, a major league team. (Robinson will go on to win the *Rookie of the Year* award, and the *Most Valuable Player* award in 1949)

	Society	Government	Sports
1947 Cont.	The first of over fifty bombings (in the next eighteen years) in Birmingham, Alabama, earning the city the tragic nickname "Bombingham."		
1948		President Truman sets up the Fair Employment Board; its role is to eliminate discrimination in federal jobs.	Negro National (Baseball) League folds, as new players join the newly integrated Major League franchises.

"There shall be equality of treatment, and opportunity for all persons in the armed services without regard to race, color, religion..."

President Truman

President Truman

	Related Military
1948 cont.	Truman makes plans to desegregate the U.S. military, signing an executive order that "there shall be equality of treatment, and opportunity for all persons in the armed services without regard to race, color, religion …." Army staff officers react by saying the order does not *prohibit* segregation in the military. Truman says in a press conference that ending segregation *is* the intent.
1949	The Army and Marine Corps defend segregation in their branches; the Navy and Air Force announce plans to integrate. Recruitment quotas (10%) are part of the Army's plan of dealing with the executive order.
1950 – 1953	U.S. involved in Korean War: "De facto" integration occurs in Army units, as black soldiers are absorbed into white units with high casualty rates.

	Happenings in Society	Government Responses	Military
1954	1,200 white businessmen meet in Selma, Alabama, organizing the White Citizens Council to protest school desegregation.	Supreme Court decision: *Brown v. Board of Education* Overturns unanimously *Plessy v. Ferguson*, and declares "separate but equal" public schools unconstitutional.	All military units are finally integrated.
1955	Rosa Parks refuses to give up her bus seat to a white man. Rosa is arrested. The Montgomery Bus Boycott begins as a result.	The Supreme Court orders lower courts to use "all deliberate speed" in desegregating schools. Alabama responds with a "pupil placement law."	

Rosa Parks   *Martin Luther King Jr.*

	Happenings in Society	**Government Responses**
1955 cont.	When fourteen-year-old Emmett Till is brutally murdered in Mississippi for "flirting with a white woman," there is a national outcry.	
1956	Dr. King is president of the new organization, "The Montgomery Improvement Association."	Southern congressmen call for resistance to Supreme Court-ordered desegregation caused by *Brown* decision.

"The unwarranted decision of the Supreme Court in the public school cases is now bearing the fruit always produced when men substitute naked power for established law."
In The Southern Manifesto, 1956

	Happenings in Society	Government Responses
1956 cont.	Montgomery's buses are desegregated after more than a year of boycotts, when the city ordinance is declared unconstitutional. (The Montgomery bus line has lost more than fifty percent of its income during the strike.) Dr. King and a white minister celebrate by riding in the front seat of a bus together.	
	When the NAACP is banned in Alabama, Reverend Shuttlesworth helps organize the Alabama Christian Movement for Human Rights (ACMHR) in its place. "They can outlaw an organization, but they can't outlaw the movement of a people determined to be free."	
1957	In response to court orders to desegregate the schools, Reverend Shuttlesworth tries to enroll his children at Phillip High School – he is beaten by a mob.	

	Happenings in Society	Government Responses	Related Military
1957 cont.	The homes of black leaders and several black churches are bombed in Montgomery.		
	When Arkansas Governor Faubus blocks black students from entering a Little Rock school (after court-ordered integration), President Eisenhower sends more than 10,000 troops to intervene.		

"The Little Rock Nine"

*"I'm the world's original gradualist.
I just think ninety-odd years is gradual enough."*
Thurgood Marshall in 1958 in response to
President Eisenhower's call for
patience in Civil Rights.

	Happenings in Society	Sports
1957 cont.		Interracial athletics are banned in Georgia by the Georgia senate.
	Dr. Martin Luther King, Jr. and Reverend Joseph E. Lowery co-found the Southern Christian Leadership Conference.	
1958	More black churches across the South are bombed.	
	Protesting school desegregation, the KKK burns eighteen crosses in Jefferson County, Alabama.	

	Happenings in Society
1958	10,000 students participate in the Youth March for Integrated Schools in Washington, D.C.
1959	Dr. King visits India, to study Gandhi's principles of nonviolence.
	Continuing to fight school segregation, the KKK parades through black neighborhoods, and burns crosses at twenty-nine schools in Jefferson County.
	In Prince Edward County, Virginia, public schools close down, rather than obey a court ordered desegregation order. (They will remain closed for five years.)

Mohandas Karamchand Gandhi

	Happenings in Society	**Government Responses**
1960	Sit-in protests start at a Woolworth's in North Carolina, when four black college students sit at a counter that will not serve blacks. The sit-ins spread across the south, to over fifty cities. They are followed up by "wade-ins" at segregated beaches and kneel-ins" at all-white churches.	President Eisenhower signs the Civil Rights Act of 1960 gives voting rights to all Americans, regardless of their skin color.
	Six years after the Supreme Court has ordered them changed, the schools in Alabama, Georgia, Mississippi, and South Carolina remain segregated.	
	Elijah Muhammad pushes for a separate all-black state within the U.S. Malcolm X will try to work with the KKK to make the idea a reality.	Reverend Martin Luther King, Jr. is arrested an jailed on yet another trumped up charge – this time it is for driving in Alabama with a Georgia license. (It is one of twenty times he will be jailed.)

	Happenings in Society	**Government Responses**
1960 cont.	After a school in New Orleans, Louisiana fights court-ordered desegregation, six-year-old Ruby Bridges becomes the first and only black student in attendance there.	Reverend Shuttlesworth's children are arrested while riding a Greyhound – the charge is violating school segregation laws.
1961	In response to new federal laws prohibiting segregation on interstate transportation, Freedom Rides begin between Washington D.C. and New Orleans. (One of the buses is set on fire by a mob in Alabama.) Several hundred black and white "freedom riders" participate over the summer, none of home make it safely to New Orleans.	President John F. Kennedy issues an executive order that creates a Committee on Equal Employment Opportunity and mentions "affirmative action" for the first time.

President Kennedy   *James Meredith*

	Happenings in Society	**Government Responses**
1961 cont.	"Jail-in": Nine sit-in demonstrators choose thirty days at hard labor, rather than paying bail.	
	City officials in Birmingham, Alabama vote to close public parks, playgrounds, and golf courses, rather than integrate them.	
1962	James Meredith enrolls as first black student at University of Mississippi. President Kennedy orders federal troops to the campus to protect him in the ensuing violence. (More than 20,000 troops are needed to stop the rioting on campus that results.)	

	Related Military	**Sport Events**
1962 Cont.	As U.S. involvement in Vietnam escalates, all military reserve units (except National Guard) are ordered integrated	Jackie Robinson is honored in the Baseball Hall of Fame.

Governor George Wallace

"The ultimate measure of a man is not where he stands in moments of comfort and convenience, but where he stands at times of challenge and controversy."
Martin Luther King, Jr.

	Happenings in Society	Government Responses
1963	Rev. Martin Luther King, Jr. and other ministers arrested for demonstrating against segregation in Birmingham, Alabama, in "Project C." King writes his famous "Letter from a Birmingham Jail" in response to the unsupportive white pastors.	George Wallace runs for governor of Alabama on the promise of "segregation now, segregation tomorrow, segregation forever."
	Two black students enroll at the University of Alabama. Governor Wallace, acting as University registrar, blocks the students from entering the school to register. President Kennedy calls out the Alabama National Guard, who order Wallace out of the way so they can enter to register.	

	Happenings in Society	**Government Responses**
1963 cont	When hundreds of black children in Birmingham, preparing for another protest march, are attacked by police with dogs and firefighters with hoses, the national outrage is tremendous.	
	The Sixteenth Street Baptist Church in Birmingham is bombed four young black girls are killed. The FBI investigates the case, identifies four suspects, and soon drops the case, claiming civil rights activists had bombed the church themselves. It will be almost forty years before charges are finally brought against the four men.	
	NAACP leader, Medgar Evers, is murdered in front of his home in Jackson, Mississippi. (The murderer is finally convicted in 1994, after a retrial.)	In response to the many civil rights violations throughout the south, President Kennedy finally comes out strongly for Civil Rights. He submits a bill that will become the Civil Rights Act of 1964.
	Rev. Martin Luther King, Jr. gives his "I Have a Dream" speech. Over 250,000 people are attending *The March on Washington* with him.	

	Happenings in Society	**Government Responses**
1963 cont		President John F. Kennedy is assassinated; Lyndon B. Johnson becomes the new president.
1964	Martin Luther King, Jr. receives Nobel Peace Prize. He is also honored as *Times* Magazine's "Man of the Year."	24th Amendment bans poll taxes for national elections.
	Three Civil Rights workers are stopped in Mississippi for speeding. They disappear and are then found murdered by the KKK. (Two were white, one was black.)	
	President Johnson signs Civil Rights Act of 1964, the most significant act of its kind to date. Segregation in public facilities and employment discrimination are both banned.	

	Government Responses	Sports
1964 cont	Massive effort to register black voters across the south through the "Freedom Summer." Much violence is associated with it, especially in Mississippi.	Cassius Clay wins the world heavy weight championship, coverts to Islam, and changes his name to Muhammad Ali.

President Johnson

	Happenings in Society	Government Responses
1965	Jimmie Lee Jackson is killed in Selma during a protest against voting rights violations.	The Voting Rights Act of 1965 is signed by President Johnson – voter tests (which were preventing minorities from voting) are completely forbidden.

	Happenings in Society
1965 Cont.	Rev. King leads three marches from Selma towards Montgomery in protest of the voting rights violations. The first attempt ends quickly on "Bloody Sunday," when fifty marchers are hospitalized after being attacked by the police. A second march two days later ends at the bridge when police brutality becomes a reality again. The third march will wait over a month, until President Johnson provides protection for the marchers, which now number in the thousands.

Bloody Sunday

The ultimate measure of a man is not where he stands in moments of comfort and convenience, but where he stands at times of challenge and controversy.
Martin Luther King, Jr.

	Happenings in Society	Government Responses
1965 cont	Race Riots lasting six days spread across Los Angeles, California.	President Johnson pushes "affirmative action" in education and jobs as a temporary measure to get minorities on an even footing.
	Malcolm X, a proponent of "non-peaceful" methods is assassinated.	The U.S. Department files suit against Mississippi for their continued use of the "poll tax" to prevent blacks from voting.
1966	The call for "Black Power" spreads through some black communities. The Black Panther Party for Self-Defense forms in response to the "Black Power" call.	President Johnson brings over 2,000 leaders together for a White House Conference on Civil Rights.
		The Civil Rights Bill of 1966 dies in the Senate after a filibuster by Southern senators.

	Happenings in Society	Government Responses
1967	Delegates at a Black Power Conference call for dividing the U.S. into two countries, one black and one white.	President Johnson appoints Thurgood Marshall (the NAACP lawyer instrumental in pursuing *Brown v. Board of Education* case) as the first black Supreme Court Justice.

Justice Thurgood Marshall

	Happenings in Society	Government Responses
1968	Thirty-nine-year-old Rev. King is assassinated in Memphis, TN. Rioting occurs in more than one hundred cities as a result.	Civil Rights Act of 1968 signed by President Johnson. It outlaws discrimination in the housing market.

"We shall overcome."

The slogan of the Civil Rights Movement, and used by President Johnson in his address to Congress about Voting Rights Issues.

	Society	Sport Events
1968		Tommie Smith and John Carlos take the Olympic victory platform barefoot to receive their gold and silver medals in the 200 meter sprint. During the U.S. National Anthem, they both give the Black Panther salute, for which they will be suspended from the U.S. team.
1969	The SNCC changes its name from Student **Nonviolent** Coordinating Committee to Student **National** Coordinating Committee.	

	Government Responses
1969 cont.	Police kill two leaders of the Black Panther Party in a raid in Chicago, Illinois.
	The FBI director, J. Edgar Hoover, declares the Black Panther Party to be "public enemy number one."
1970	Governors in Alabama, Florida, Georgia, and Louisiana vow to fight school desegregation.
1971	Supreme Court Decision: *Swann v. Charlotte-Mecklenburg Board of Education*. Court-ordered Busing is upheld as legitimate method of integrating schools.

	Sports
1974	Hank Aaron surpasses Babe Ruth's Major League home run record. He will receive much hate mail from whites as a result.

	Sports
1976	Jesse Owens is awarded the *Medal of Freedom* by President Ford.

President Gerald Ford

	Happenings in Society	**Government Responses**
1978	*Regents of the University of California v. Bakke*: A white male sues for "reverse discrimination" when his application for medical school is turned down two years in a row. The Supreme Court rules in a close decision that "inflexible quotas" are illegal, but leaves room for "affirmative action" to a point.	
1982		Wallace wins fourth term as governor of Alabama, this time running on a platform of racial and religious tolerance.

	Government Responses
1983	President Regan signs law making Martin Luther King Jr.'s birthday a national holiday. (It will be observed nationally for the first time in 1986.)

President Ronald Reagan

	Happenings in Society	Government Responses	Sports
1990	Nelson Mandela is released from prison in South Africa where he has spent twenty-eight years for opposing apartheid.		The NFL cancels its plans to hold the 1993 Super Bowl in Arizona because the state refuses to honor Martin Luther King, Jr. Day.

	Happenings in Society	Government Responses
1991	The NAACP opposes President Bush's nomination of Clarence Thomas to the Supreme Court – because Thomas is to conservative.	
1992	Four white police officers are acquitted after beating Rodney King, a black motorist (an act that had been videotaped and televised). Race riots spread across the city. More than fifty deaths and 17,000 arrests will occur during the three days of rioting.	
1995		Affirmative Action receives a blow when the U.S. Supreme Court rules that preferential treatment based on any race is almost always unconstitutional.
1997		Proposition 209 passes in California, the first state to thus end affirmative action: discrimination and preferential treatment of any kind are disallowed.

	Happenings in Society	Government Responses
2003		The U.S. Supreme Court allows the University of Michigan to continue to encourage minority law school applicants, but strikes down its point system that favors minorities in undergraduate admission.
2007	The Supreme Court reaffirms that the government has a compelling interest in educational diversity at the same time it rules against the current use of race to determine school placement in Louisville, KY and Seattle, WA.	
2008	In what is seen by many as a historic civil rights victory, citizens of the United States elect the first black man as President of the United States.	

Conclusion

May this little booklet motivate you to learn more about this important part of our country's past (and present)!

If you would like more information on the Civil Rights, there are countless websites and books available on the subject. The book I found that was the most eye-opening to me as I did my research was: *Civil Rights Chronicle, the African-American Struggle for Freedom*. It is a huge book, over 400 pages. The pictures in it alone are an education on this important topic!

To actually "see and feel" many of the events and people of the Civil Rights Movement, I also recommend the *Birmingham Civil Rights Institute*, (http://www.bcri.org/index.html), right off I-65 and I-20/59, in downtown Birmingham. It brought things to life in a remarkable way.

May we not be content to just let things be, when changes are needed, taking to heart Martin Luther King, Jr.'s words:

"True peace is not merely the absence of tension; it is the presence of justice."

"Injustice anywhere is a threat to justice everywhere."

Martin Luther King, Jr.

Notes